the story of the U.S.A.
by Franklin Escher, Jr.

Book 2
A Young Nation Solves Its Problems

Educators Publishing Service
Cambridge and Toronto

Printed in USA

ISBN 978-0-8388-1633-2

16 PAH 12

Table of Contents

For the Student

Welcome to the world of American history. You are going to read about our country's past. History is filled with exciting stories and interesting people. This book will tell you about some of them. It can also help you practice ways to read and study that you can use in all your classes, not just in history class.

Before you start working in this book, you will need to know how it is put together. Each chapter is arranged into parts that take you along one step at a time. If you follow the directions, you will be able to read and learn the material without any trouble.

To begin with, there are pictures and sometimes maps at the start of each chapter. By studying them, you will get an idea of what you are going to be reading about.

Next, there are a few vocabulary words. This vocabulary section gives meanings and pronunciations for some words that will appear in the chapter. The letters in CAPITALS are parts of the word which are accented, or said the loudest:

example = eg-ZAM-pul

Turn next to the chapter story. At the beginning are two or three questions, just beneath the title. These give you some hints about the main ideas and help you start thinking *before* you read. Keep these questions in mind, and look for the answers as you read.

Some words in the chapter story are printed in heavy black type called **boldface**. These are the words from the vocabulary page. Some other words and names are printed in *italics*. That is a signal to look at the right-hand column of the page if you need help in pronouncing them.

One more thing to look for is a black dot ●. Most chapters are divided into sections, with a dot to show that a main section has come to an end. That should be your signal to stop and think back over the paragraphs in that section. Try to tell yourself the main ideas that were built up. Ask yourself WHAT happened, WHO did it, and WHY. A quick review like this helps you take the facts and ideas from a book and put them into your own words. That is the best way of all to study.

At the end of each chapter you will find exercises to do. Don't think of these as a test. They are designed to help you review the most important facts and ideas in the chapter. As you work along through the book, think carefully about what you are reading. This will help you to do the exercises without having to look back at the chapter.

Exercise A always deals with the main ideas. Ideas are even more important than facts. If you know the main ideas of a story, you understand its meaning. For example, it is just as important to know *why* France sold Louisiana to the United States as it is to know *when* it was done.

Exercise C, D, or E is a vocabulary review. This exercise should be easy. It is designed to help you strengthen and build your vocabulary by giving you extra practice with the words from the first page of the chapter. You will see some of those words again and again in later parts of the book. The last exercise in each chapter is called "Think About and Discuss in Class." Here, you and your classmates can begin to relate the past to the present and to your own lives. You can look for the lessons that history can teach us. Why do wars start? Why do people starve? How can the world be made a happier place to live in?

History teaches us lessons, and it is fun to read. You'll enjoy the stories of the first explorers and settlers of America. Some of them were heroes, some villains, and some were a little of both. Pick out your favorites and talk about them in class.

As you turn these pages, you will find yourself reading faster and faster. Keep it up! Within a short time, you will be moving easily through this book. It will help make you a better reader and a better student.

Angry farmers in Massachusetts revolted against the government in Shays' Rebéllion.

Under the Articles of Confederation, Congress did not have its own money. Each state printed money for itself.

Getting Ready for Chapter One

1

Here are five vocabulary words that are used in the story of the first United States government. Study these definitions so you will know what each word means when you see it in your reading.

Congress	(KON-gress) A council of men and women that makes laws for a country.
confederation	(kun-fed-er-AY-shun) States or countries that work together as a group but keep their own independence.
bayonet	(BAY-uh-net) A long knife attached to the end of a rifle.
rebellion	(re-BEL-yun) A fight or revolt against a government.
delegate	(DEL-uh-gut) A representative. A person chosen to speak for others.

The Articles of Confederation were weak because Congress could not:

1.
Raise or collect taxes;

2.
Raise an army;

3.
Make treaties with foreign countries;

4.
Control foreign trade and tariffs;

5.
Control trade among the states.

The weak government of the Articles of Confederation was causing more and more problems. Congress had little power over the states. States were quarreling among themselves, business was bad, and times were hard.

Our First Government

What was the first government of the United States like?
Why did Americans want that kind of government?
How well did the first government work?

Suppose you are in a basketball game where there is no teamwork. Each player tries to make a basket without passing the ball to anyone else. How well do you think your team will do? Will it be able to score many points?

Our country faced the problem of not enough teamwork two hundred years ago. The thirteen American colonies joined together in 1775 to win independence from England. Each colony sent representatives to a meeting at Philadelphia. The group of representatives was called **Congress.** They wrote a plan of government called the *Articles* of **Confederation.** Using this plan, Congress set up the first government of the United States of America. From then on, the thirteen colonies were called states.

AR-tih-kulz

During the Revolution, Congress asked the thirteen states to send soldiers and money for the war. Sometimes the states sent help. Sometimes they didn't. Congress needed every state's help, but it did not have *power* to TELL them what to do. The American government under the Articles of Confederation was very weak. •

POW-ur

Thanks to George Washington's leadership and to help from France, the United States became free in 1781. But the country still had a weak government. The trouble was that the American people did not want a strong one! They had fought and died for freedom from England. Now they felt that a strong Congress would be as bad as a strong king.

Congress had no money. It had borrowed cash from other countries to fight the war. Afterward, the American government was so poor that it could not pay its army. Angry soldiers pushed **bayonets** through the windows of the *building* where Congress met. The frightened Congressmen quickly left Philadelphia. •

BIL-ding

Meanwhile, the thirteen states were acting like thirteen different nations. Each state had its own government and printed its own money. The states *quarreled* and fought among themselves. They refused to buy each other's goods because times were hard. Banks and businesses closed. Stores shut their doors.

KWAR-uld

Serious trouble broke out in Massachusetts. The farmers there were very poor. They thought taxes were too high. Many of them owed money to merchants and bankers. The merchants said they would take away the farmers' land if they did not pay what they owed.

SEE-ree-uss

Led by Captain Daniel Shays, who had fought in the Revolution, the farmers revolted. They attacked some towns in Massachusetts. Then they tried to *capture* guns the U.S. government stored at Springfield. The government could not send soldiers to protect its own property. The governor of Massachusetts then called out state troops to stop the revolt. Shays' **Rebellion** was put down in 1787. •

KAP-chur

By now, people in all thirteen states were worried about what was happening to the country. The United States was falling apart. George Washington and other leaders called for a stronger government. It was the only way to save the nation.

Congress finally did something. It called a meeting at Philadelphia of **delegates** from all the states. The delegates would discuss ways to change the Articles of Confederation.

Answer these to review the main ideas.

A.

1. What were the Articles of Confederation? _____

_____

Did this plan of government give Congress much power? _____

_____

2. What problems did Congress have in trying to run the country? ___

_____

_____

How did the thirteen states behave? _____

_____

_____

3. What kind of government did the American people want at first?

_____

Why did they feel this way? _____

_____

_____

Circle the right answer to finish each sentence.

1. The American colonies fought for independence from

   a. France   b. Spain   c. England

2. The thirteen colonies became

   a. states   b. provinces   c. counties

3. The American Revolution ended in

   a. 1775   b. 1776   c. 1781

4. The Americans said that a strong Congress would be as bad as a

   a. strong king   b. weak king   c. confederation

5. The leader of the Massachusetts farmers' revolt was

   a. George Washington   b. Daniel Shays   c. the governor of Massachusetts

Circle True or False.

T F 1. Congress got money to pay for the war by taxing the people.

T F 2. The representatives wrote a plan of government called the Articles of Confederation.

T F 3. The thirteen states always obeyed orders given by Congress.

T F 4. The states got along very well together.

T F 5. Congress asked for a meeting to change the Articles of Confederation.

Choose one of these words to fit each sentence below.

Congress   confederation   bayonet

rebellion   delegate

1. A group of countries or states that works together under a weak central government is called a _____.

2. Each state sent _____s to a meeting at Philadelphia.

3. Soldiers sometimes have _____s attached to the ends of their guns or rifles.

4. The group of representatives which made laws for the United States was called _____.

5. When people fight against their own government, they are staging a _____.

Think about and discuss in class.

E.

This chapter talks about teamwork. Which would you rather be — a big star on a losing team, or a poor player on a winning team? Why?

_____

_____

_____

Daniel Shays was pardoned after leading the farmers' rebellion in Massachusetts. Shays had used violence against the people of that state. Why do you think he was let off so easily? _____

_____

Under the Articles of Confederation, the United States had a Congress, but no president. Try to imagine what it would be like if we had no president today. What extra jobs would Congress have to do?

_____

_____

_____

_____

_____

_____

_____

_____

_____

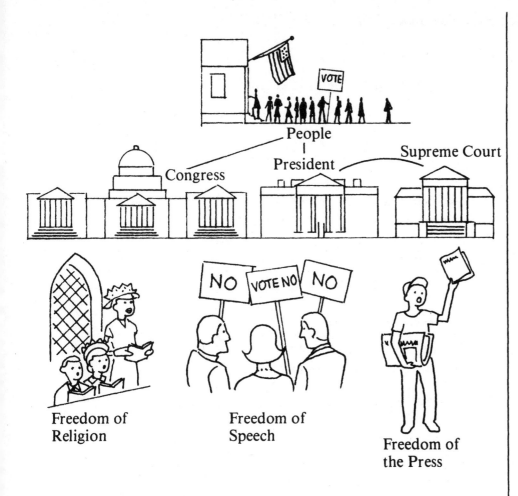

People

Congress

President

Supreme Court

Freedom of
Religion

Freedom of
Speech

Freedom of
the Press

The Constitution set up three branches of government to run the country. Each branch has some power over the others, so one branch can not get too important. This is called the system of checks and balances.

The first ten amendments to the Constitution are called the Bill of Rights. They give Americans important freedoms.

Getting Ready for Chapter Two

2

Here are six vocabulary words that are used in the story about a new plan of government. Study these definitions so you will know what each word means when you see it in your reading.

convention   (kun-VEN-shun)   A meeting where delegates get together for a special reason.

compromise   (KOM-pruh-myz)   The ending of an argument by having both sides give in a little.

federation   (fed-ur-AY-shun)   A group of states that works together and agrees to obey a strong central or "federal" government.

supreme   (soo-PREÉM)   Highest, greatest.

minimum   (MIN-uh-mum)   Lowest, least.

veto   (VEE-tow)   The power of the president to refuse to sign bills sent by Congress. But if Congress passes the same bill again by a vote of two-thirds of its members, it becomes a law anyway.

Confederation and Federation

No Leader

Strong Leader

Won't Pay Taxes

Must Pay Taxes

Weak Army

Strong Army

Under the new Constitution our government was a federation of states. It was stronger than it was under the Articles of Confederation.

A New Plan of Government

What caused an argument between the large and small states?
How did they settle the argument?
What is the difference between a confederation and a federation?
Which is more powerful — a state government or the federal government?   Why?

In the boiling hot summer of 1787, American leaders planned a new kind of government for the United States. The plan they finally agreed on was called the *Constitution*. It is still in use today and will probably last for centuries.

kon-stih-TOO-shun

Congress wanted changes made in the Articles of Confederation. But the delegates who came to Philadelphia were tired of the weak Articles. They threw them aside, like a worn-out shoe. Then they planned a brand new government that was much stronger.

The delegates chose George Washington to run their **convention**. Other *famous* men who helped were Benjamin Franklin of Pennsylvania, John Adams of Massachusetts, and Alexander Hamilton of New York. James Madison of Virginia kept a record of everything that was said at the convention.

FAY-muss

As soon as the meeting started, trouble began. The big states and the small states could not get along. States like Virginia and Pennsylvania wanted the largest number of votes in Congress because they had the most people. But small states like New Jersey thought they should have as much power as the big states.

After a long quarrel, the two sides reached a **compromise**. There would be a new Congress. It would be divided into two parts, called houses. In the House of Representatives, the states with the most people would have the most members. But in the *Senate* every state, large or small, would have two senators and two votes.

SEH-nut

This bargain, called the Great Compromise, pleased everyone. The delegates settled down to write the rest of the Constitution. They finished it in September 1787. •

The men who met at Philadelphia changed our government from a confederation to a **federation**. As you know, a confederation is a group of *separate* states. The states are tied loosely together by a weak central government. They do not have to obey that government.

SEP-rit

A federation is much stronger. The states agree to give up some of their power. The federal government is then stronger than the state governments. The states and their citizens have to obey the federal government in many important matters.

No matter what state we live in, the federal government is important in our lives. For example, the federal government prints the money we use. It makes sure that the food we eat and the *medicines* we take are pure. If we break a federal law, we can be put on trial in a federal court. If we are found guilty, we can be sent to a federal prison. And every year we must pay the government in Washington, D.C., a tax on the money we earn.

MED-ih-sinz

The delegates at Philadelphia kept some powers for the states. State governments run their own public schools. They build roads and highways. They have their own police and make their own traffic and criminal laws. But as the Constitution says, "This Constitution and the laws of the United States ... shall be the **supreme** law of the land; and the judges in every state shall be bound thereby." •

The United States government set up by the Constitution is made up of three parts or "branches." The first part is Congress, the *legislative* branch. Congress makes laws for people in all the states. The second part is the president, the *executive* branch. The president of the United States sees that the laws are carried out. The third part is the Supreme Court, the *judicial* branch. The Supreme Court acts as the highest court for federal law cases. It also judges whether or not the laws follow the Constitution.

LEJ-iss-lay-tiv
egs-ECK-you-tiv

joo-DISH-ul

The Constitution gives Congress many powers. The Congress makes laws. It borrows money by selling government bonds to the people. It manages our armed forces — the Navy, the Army, and the Air Force. It sets **minimum** wages that employers must pay workers. And it controls the prices that airlines, railroads, and trucks may charge the public.

The president is *commander*-in-chief, or the highest leader, of the armed forces. He also takes care of our dealings with foreign countries and makes *treaties*, if the Senate agrees. He appoints important *officials*. He suggests laws that he thinks will help the country. He can **veto** laws he thinks are not good ideas. He is elected by the people in all of the states.

kuh-MAN-dur

TREE-teez
o-FISH-ulz

The Supreme Court can judge the laws Congress passes. It uses the Constitution to decide what kind of laws the United States may have. If the Court thinks a law goes against the rules of the Constitution, it can set it aside. Then it is no longer a law.

Each branch of the government has some power over the other two. This system is called the system of checks and balances. One branch of government can check—or stop—some of the things another branch does. The purpose is to keep the government well balanced, making it very difficult for any one part to seize control. •

To keep the Constitution fresh and useful, the American people can make changes in it. These changes are called amendments. More than twenty-five amendments have already been made. The first ten were added in 1791. These ten amendments are called the Bill of Rights. They *guarantee* Americans such rights as freedom of speech, freedom of religion, and freedom of the press.

gar-un-TEE

After the Constitution was written in 1787, it had to be *ratified* (agreed to) by the states. As soon as nine states ratified it, the United States would have a strong new government.

RAT-uh-fide

This happened in 1788, but many Americans were still afraid of a strong federal government. They wanted to be sure the rights of each person were protected. Therefore, when many of the states ratified the Constitution, they said the Bill of Rights should be part of it too. Finally, in 1790, all thirteen states had ratified the Constitution, and in 1791, as the states had asked, the Bill of Rights was added.

The new government was strong, but the people still had a lot of power. They could elect representatives they thought would be good leaders, and they could vote against people they did not like. In 1788, the Constitution became the law of the land, and it still is.

Answer these to review the main ideas.

A.

1. What happened to the Articles of Confederation? _____

_____

2. What was the argument between the large and small states in 1787?

_____

_____

How was the problem solved? _____

_____

_____

3. Which is stronger, a federation or a confederation? _____

_____

Why? _____

_____

4. What are the parts or branches of the federal government? _____

_____

5. What does the system of checks and balances do? _____

_____

Circle True or False.

T F 1. The delegates at Philadelphia wanted to keep the Articles of Confederation.

T F 2. The large states and small states did not get along well together at first.

T F 3. Every state, large or small, has two senators in the Senate.

T F 4. Every state, large or small, has the same number of representatives in the House of Representatives.

T F 5. The federal government cannot punish the citizens of a state.

Circle the right answer to finish each sentence.

1. The person chosen to run the convention was

   a. George   b. James Madison   c. Alexander
      Washington   Hamilton

2. Federal laws are made by

   a. the president   b. Congress   c. the states

3. The commander-in-chief of the armed forces is

   a. the Supreme Court b. Congress   c. the president

4. The first ten amendments are called the

   a. confederation   b. Bill of Rights c. government

5. The delegates gave the states

   a. the right to do   b. some powers   c. no powers
      anything they
      pleased

Choose one of these words to fit each sentence below.

supreme   federation   veto

compromise   minimum   convention

1. When two sides settle an argument by each giving in a little, they

   make a _____.

2. The president of the United States can _____ bills

   from Congress that he doesn't like.

3. When states give up some of their power to a federal government, they become a _____.

4. The least amount of money a worker can be paid is the _____ wage.

5. The Constitution is the _____ law of the United States.

6. The men who wrote the Constitution held a _____ at Philadelphia.

Think about and discuss in class.

What is a compromise? Have you ever made a compromise with someone? Explain. _____

_____

_____

If Congress passes a law that some people do not like, what can those people do about it? _____

_____

Why is the Bill of Rights important to Americans? _____

_____

_____

Thomas Jefferson was secretary of state, in charge of foreign affairs. He was a member of Washington's cabinet.

Our first president was George Washington. He was the hero of the Revolution and was loved and trusted by the American people.

America's first capital was New York. Washington took office there.

Getting Ready for Chapter Three

Here are three vocabulary words that are used in the story of our first president. Study these definitions so that you will know what each word means when you see it in your reading.

statesman   (STAYTS-mun)   A person in the government who is a leader in national and world affairs.

population   (pop-yoo-LAY-shun)   The number of people living in a place, such as a city or a country.

neutral   (NOO-trul)   Not taking a side in an argument. Keeping out of a fight or war.

Our First President and His Times

Who thought that rich men should run our country?
Who thought that working people should have the
most power?
What did President Washington say we should do about
wars in Europe?

Everyone knew who the first president of the United States would
be. The American people voted for General George Washington of
Virginia, the hero of the Revolution. John Adams of Massachusetts
was chosen vice-president.

George Washington did not want to be president. He was a soldier,
not a **statesman**. He hated to make speeches. But he knew he must
serve, because the American people wanted him. The country needed
a leader it felt it could trust.

New York City was our country's first capital. When he arrived
there, Washington was cheered by big crowds. People waved flags.
Church bells rang out the good news. Cannons boomed. There was a
great celebration when America's first president took office in 1789. •

The United States was a small country then. It had fewer than 4
million settlers. Today, our **population** is about 250 million. That
means that for each American living in 1789, there are over sixty
Americans today.

MIL-yun

George Washington chose some advisers to help him with all the
work he had to do. This group of advisers was called the cabinet. Each
cabinet member was called a *secretary*, and had a *special* job to do.

SEH-kreh-tair-ee SPEH-shu

Washington picked *Alexander* Hamilton to be secretary of the
treasury. Hamilton had served in the army with Washington all
through the Revolution. He had been a hero at the Battle of
Yorktown. •

al-eg-ZAN-dur

As head of the treasury, Hamilton was in charge of money affairs.
Our country was very poor because the states had *refused* to pay taxes
to the old government. Hamilton said that the new government was
strong enough to collect the money it needed from the states. He also
believed that the country should be run by rich bankers and merchants. He thought that since they could build factories and make
cities grow, they should have the most power.

ree-FYOOZD

Many Americans were shocked at this idea. They did not think it
was fair. One of these people was Thomas Jefferson, who had written
most of the Declaration of Independence. Jefferson was also a
member of President Washington's cabinet. As secretary of state, he
was in charge of foreign affairs.

Although he was quite rich himself, Jefferson disagreed with Hamilton. Jefferson believed that America should be run by the farmers and storekeepers. There were a lot more of them than there were of the rich people. "Those who labor in the earth are the chosen people of God," Jefferson declared. There were some strong *arguments* between Jefferson and Hamilton at cabinet meetings.

AR-gyoo-mentz

The United States was planning to build a new capital. Northerners wanted it to be in the North. Southerners were eager to have it in the South. Jefferson was a Southerner.

Hamilton offered Jefferson a bargain. "If you Southerners will vote for my tax program," Hamilton said, "I'll get Northerners to vote for putting the new capital in the South." Jefferson agreed, and Congress passed both plans. Washington, our capital, is in the District of Columbia. The southern states gave land for the city to be built on. Washington, D.C., became the capital of the United States in 1800. •

While George Washington was president, our young nation faced danger from abroad. England and France were at war on land and at sea. The British captured American ships carrying supplies to France. The French urged us to help them defeat England because France had helped us in the Revolution.

George Washington remained *calm*. America's best hope, he said, was to keep out of wars in Europe. During his two terms as president, America stayed **neutral**.

KAHM

George Washington left office in 1797 and went home to Virginia. He had given a lifetime of good service to his country.

Answer these to review the main ideas.

A.

1. Why didn't George Washington want to be president of the United States? _____

2. What were Alexander Hamilton's ideas about how we should run the country? _____

_____

What were Thomas Jefferson's ideas? _____

_____

3. How did Hamilton manage to get his tax program passed by Congress?_____

_____

Circle the right answer to finish each sentence. B.

1. Our nation's first capital was

   a. Boston   b. New York   c. Washington

2. Our population in 1789 was about

   a. 40 million   b. 4 million   c. 225 million

3. The group of people who advise the president is called

   a. the cabinet   b. the Senate   c. Congress

4. Washington's secretary of the treasury was

   a. Thomas Jefferson   b. John Adams   c. Alexander Hamilton

5. While Washington was president, England was fighting with

   a. Germany   b. France   c. Spain

Circle True or False. C.

T   F   1. The American people did not like George Washington.

T   F   2. Thomas Jefferson did not think American farmers were important.

T   F   3. Washington, our capital, is located in Virginia.

T   F   4. The British captured American ships carrying goods to the French.

T   F   5. George Washington served two terms as president.

Choose one of these words to fit each sentence below. D.

population   neutral   statesman

1. A government leader in national or foreign affairs is a

   _____.

2. When we do not take sides in a war, we are _____.

3. The number of people living in a place is the _____.

Think about and discuss in class. E.

Why did the French expect us to help them in their war with England?

_____

_____

Why do you think the North and the South both wanted the new capital to be built in their part of the country? _____

_____

_____

Alexander Hamilton wanted America to be a land of factories and cities. Thomas Jefferson wanted it to be a land of small farms. Whose wishes came closer to being true? _____

_____

George Washington died in 1799. Name a committee to find out what he died of. How did the doctors try to help him? If Washington had lived in our time, do you think the doctors would have been able to save him? How? _____

_____

_____

Captain Robert Gray explored the Columbia River in Oregon. Because of his trip, America claimed the Oregon country.

Missions were places where priests and friars taught the Native Americans the Christian religion.

Ships from New York had to sail all the way around South America to reach the Pacific Ocean and China. How do ships get there now?

Getting Ready for Chapter Four

4

Here are five vocabulary words that are used in the story about settling the Pacific Coast. Study these definitions so you will know what each word means when you see it in your reading.

developed   (duh-VEL-upt)   Grown into a more organized way of living.

mission   (MISH-un)   A place where people do religious work and teach their religion to others.

adobe   (uh-DOE-bee)   Bricks made of clay and straw and baked in the sun.

friar   (FRY-ur)   A member of a religious group in the Roman Catholic church. A monk.

Yankee   (YANG-kee)   A person who lives in the United States, especially a Northerner.

Settlements on the Pacific Coast

During George Washington's time the United States reached only from the Atlantic coast west to the Mississippi River.
What kind of civilization did the Spanish find when they started a colony in California?
What brought Americans to the Pacific Coast?

For over two hundred years Spain had claimed California, but had not started any colonies. Many different Native Americans had been living there for centuries, however, and had built well-**developed** civilizations. ●

Spain decided to start a colony in California when it began to worry that England and Russia might challenge its claim. The Russians, who were exploring Oregon and Alaska, were very near. So King Charles of Spain ordered Spanish soldiers to go to the coast of California. They went by land and by sea. They built a chain of forts and **missions** there.

One of the people who did most to settle California for Spain was a Roman Catholic priest named *Junipero Serra*. Father Serra wanted to teach Native Americans his own religious faith. The Spanish leaders wanted the Native Americans to work for them and learn the Spanish way of life as well.

hoo-NEE-peh-row SER-uh

Father Serra helped build twenty-one missions from San Diego to San Francisco. (The mission at San Francisco was started in 1776.) They were spaced twenty-five miles apart along a trail called *El Camino Real*. In English this means The King's Highway. The missions were built of yellow bricks called **adobe**. Each mission had a church and buildings where Native Americans lived. Native Americans had to help the people in the mission with the farming and the everyday work that had to be done. Priests and **friars** there tried to convert them to the Christian religion. The Native American way of life was totally changed. Thousands died of diseases brought by white men.

el kuh-MEEN-ow ray-AHL

In 1784, the year Father Serra died, an American ship sailed out of New York. It was called the *Empress of China*. The ship sailed half way around the world and docked in Canton, China. There the Americans traded medicine for Chinese tea and silk.

This was the beginning of the China trade. It brought Americans from the east coast out west to the Pacific coast. Ships from Boston and

New York had to sail all the way around South America to reach the Pacific Ocean (see map, p. 21).

Yankee traders from New England sailed thousands of miles to Oregon. They got furs from the Native Americans there. Then they took the furs all the way across the Pacific Ocean to China. They sold them in Asia for very high prices.

In 1792 a Boston sea captain named Robert Gray sailed along the Oregon coast. Gray found a big river that he named after his ship, the *Columbia*. As a result of this trip, the United States claimed the Oregon country.

In 1800 the populations on both sides of North America were growing. The Atlantic coast was part of the United States. California belonged to Spain, and Alaska to the Russians. But Americans were doing business on the Pacific coast. Some dreamed of the day when the American flag would fly over both coasts, from ocean to ocean.

Answer these to review the main ideas.   A.

1. What nations threatened California? What did Spain do about it?

_____

_____

2. What two important events in American history happened in 1776?

_____

3. Who was Father Serra? _____

_____

   What did he do? _____

_____

_____

4. Why did American traders go to Oregon? _____

_____

_____

5. How did the United States happen to claim the Oregon country?

_____

_____

Circle True or False.

T F 1. Spain was afraid that the Russians were going to move into Spanish territory.

T F 2. American ships going to Oregon had to sail all the way around South America.

T F 3. Furs from Oregon brought high prices in Asia.

T F 4. The *Empress of China* was an American ship that sailed all the way to Canton, China.

Circle the right answer to finish each sentence.

1. Alaska was once owned by

   a. Russia   b. Spain   c. England

2. The number of missions Father Serra built in California was

   a. 21   b. 100   c. 2100

3. El Camino Real means

   a. His Royal Highness   b. the King's Highway   c. the real thing

4. Traders sold Native American furs in

   a. California   b. Asia   c. New York

5. The missions were built of

   a. adobe   b. wood   c. stone

6. The river explored by Captain Robert Gray was the

   a. Mississippi   b. Columbia   c. Snake

Choose one of these words to fit each sentence below.

mission   adobe   friar   Yankee   developed

1. Sun-dried bricks made of clay and straw are called _____.

2. A place where people work to spread their religion is called a

   _____.

3. Americans, especially Northerners, are often called _____s.

4. Monks and other members of Roman Catholic religious orders are

   known as _____s.

5. The small town _____ into a big city.

Think about and discuss in class.

Name some of the things that Spain and her old colonies have given to the United States of America. Start with Spanish words in our language. Then name some Spanish foods that Americans enjoy. What cities, rivers, and mountains have Spanish names? What about Spanish dances and music? How many people speak Spanish in the

city or town that you live in? _____

_____

_____

_____

_____

_____

_____

If you were to sail on a ship from the West coast to New York today,

what route would you take? _____

Would you have to sail around the tip of South America? _____
If you need to, look at a map.

If you live west of the Mississippi River, write down the names of as many big cities and rivers in the East as you can. If you live east of the Mississippi River, write down the names of as many big cities and rivers in the West as you can.

East	West
_____	_____
_____	_____
_____	_____
_____	_____
_____	_____
_____	_____

Jefferson bought the Louisiana Territory from France for 15 million dollars. The land doubled the size of the United States.

Napoleon was the ruler of France. He wanted to take back the land that France had lost in North America.

Toussaint L'Ouverture led the Black slaves in Haiti. They defeated Napoleon's army and Haiti became a free nation.

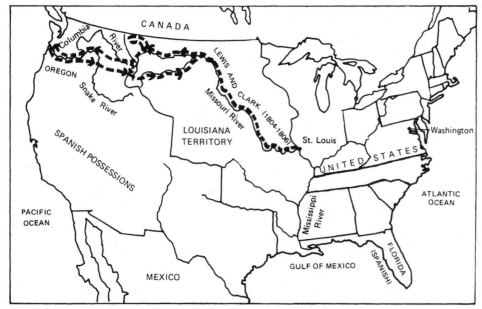

Jefferson sent Lewis and Clark to explore the Louisiana Territory. They started from St. Louis and went across the Rocky Mountains to the Pacific Ocean.

A Native American woman named Sacajawea helped guide Lewis and Clark on their expedition west.

Getting Ready for Chapter Five

5

Here are four vocabulary words that are used in the story about exploring the West. Study these definitions so you will know what each word means when you see it in your reading.

ambassador (am-BASS-uh-dur) A government official who represents his or her country in a foreign nation.

territory (TER-ih-TOR-ee) A partly settled area of land belonging to a government.

purchase (PUR-chuss) To buy.

frontier (frun-TEER) The border between settled or populated lands and unsettled lands or wilderness.

Exploring the West

Why did France sell Louisiana to the United States?
Why did President Jefferson send an expedition to Louisiana?
How far west did the expedition travel?

Thomas Jefferson became our third president in 1801. He wanted to be thought of as a plain American, not as a ruler or king. Jefferson dressed simply. He walked on the streets of Washington instead of riding in a big *carriage*. He once shocked the British **ambassador** by greeting him in a bathrobe and slippers. •

KAR-ij

In Europe, France was at war with several countries. The French ruler was named *Napoleon*. He was a proud man who wanted to beat England and take back lands that France had lost in North America. One of these lands was Louisiana, which had been taken over by Spain. Louisiana was a **territory** next door to the United States.

nuh-POW-lee-un

Napoleon forced Spain to give him back Louisiana. Next he sent a large army to the French colony of *Haiti* in the West Indies. He ordered it to stop a rebellion of Black slaves there. Then it was to move into Louisiana. The American people were very worried about having the French army move so close to them.

HAY-tee

But the French army in Haiti was in for a surprise. The Black slaves and their leader, *Toussaint L'Ouverture*, defeated the French. Many French soldiers died in the hot climate. Napoleon's army was beaten. Haiti became a free Black nation. •

TOO-san loo-vur-TYOOR

Napoleon had to make new plans. He was spending too much money on war. Why not sell Louisiana? Then France would be rich enough to defeat its enemies.

President Jefferson guessed what Napoleon was thinking. Through his ambassadors, he offered to buy New Orleans, a city in Louisiana, for 2 million dollars, not knowing that the French had offered to sell the U.S. all of Louisiana for 15 million dollars. The ambassadors agreed to the sale, but Jefferson worried that the U.S. might not have the right to buy new territory. He also felt this was too great an opportunity to miss. The treaty was announced in Washington on July 4, 1833.

HYOOJ

The Louisiana territory was *huge*. It was much larger than the state of Louisiana is now. It stretched from the Mississippi River all the way to the Rocky Mountains. No one was sure what its exact size was. So President Jefferson sent an expedition to find out. He wanted to learn as much as he could about the land he had bought. •

The Lewis and Clark Expedition started out from St. Louis, *Missouri*, in 1804. There were forty men, most of them soldiers. Clark brought along his slave, a man named York. The expedition rowed boats north up the Missouri River to North Dakota. It spent the winter there.

miz-OOR-ee

The native people had seen white trappers before, but never a Black man like York. They got along better with him than with anyone else.

Lewis and Clark had good luck on their trip. On their way west they met a French trapper and his young Native American wife and baby son. Her name was *Sacajawea*, which means "Bird Woman." The couple joined the expedition as *guides*.

SAK-a-ja-WEE-uh
GYDZ

The explorers went high into the dangerous Rocky Mountains on foot and on horseback. One day Sacajawea met her brother, whom she had not seen in many years. He had become a chief. That meant the expedition would have more friendly help in its travels.

After climbing the Rockies, Lewis and Clark had crossed the Louisiana territory. Then they floated west down the mighty Columbia River. In November 1805, they stood on the Oregon coast looking at the wide Pacific Ocean. It was the first time in history that white men had crossed the American continent.

One year later Lewis and Clark were back in St. Louis. They sent back maps and reports of their trip to President Jefferson, who was pleased. The land in the Louisiana **Purchase** doubled the size of the United States. •

More expeditions were sent to explore the West. One of them was captured by Spaniards when it got into New Mexico. Fur traders built trading posts in the Oregon country and again claimed Oregon for the United States.

Our country had moved a long way in just a few years. Thomas Jefferson had pushed the American **frontier** from the Mississippi River to the Pacific coast. Americans could now reach the Pacific by both land and sea.

Answer these to review the main ideas.

A.

1. Who was Napoleon? What were his war plans? _____

_____

_____

2. Why did Napoleon have to change his plans? _____

_____

_____

3. Why did President Jefferson send Lewis and Clark on an

   expedition to the West? _____

_____

_____

4. Where did Lewis and Clark begin their trip? How far west did they go? _____

_____

_____

5. How did the Lewis and Clark Expedition help the United States?

_____

_____

B. **Circle the right answer to finish each sentence.**

1. The leader of the Black slaves in Haiti was

   a. Napoleon   b. Toussaint   c. Sacajawea
                           L'Ouverture

2. The United States bought Louisiana from

   a. France   b. England   c. Spain

3. The price paid for Louisiana was only

   a. 5 million dollars b. 5 billion dollars c. 15 million dollars

4. The Lewis and Clark Expedition both started and ended at

   a. New York   b. St. Louis   c. Oregon

5. The young Native American woman who helped Lewis and Clark was named

   a. Pocahontas   b. Toussaint   c. Sacajawea

6. As a result of the Louisiana Purchase, the United States

   a. tripled in size   b. doubled in size   c. stayed the
                                                 same size

C. **Circle True or False.**

T F 1. Thomas Jefferson wanted people to think of him as a plain American.

T F 2. The American people were glad to welcome the French back to Louisiana.

T F 3. The French army conquered Haiti and moved into Louisiana.

T F 4. The Louisiana territory stretched from the Mississippi River to the Rocky Mountains.

30

T F 5. American explorers who went into New Mexico were captured by the Spaniards.

T F 6. Native Americans had seen many Black people.

Choose one of these words to fit each sentence below.

territory   ambassador   purchase   frontier

1. A statesman sent from a foreign country to represent it in the United States is called its _____.

2. The line between the western border of the United States and the wilderness beyond was called the _____.

3. When we buy or pay for something, we _____ it.

4. Louisiana was once a _____ of the United States.

Think about and discuss in class.

How did Lewis and Clark travel across the continent? _____

_____

Native Americans especially liked Clark's slave, York. Can you think why? _____

_____

Is the United States doing any exploring now? Where? _____

_____

The British navy stopped American ships trading with Europe. They also kidnaped American sailors and forced them to work on British ships.

Andrew Jackson and his troops defeated the British at New Orleans. This surprise victory took place after the two sides had agreed to stop fighting! Why? Could such a mistake happen today?

Francis Scott Key watched the American flag flying over the fort defending Baltimore against the British. It gave him the idea for the "Star-Spangled Banner."

Getting Ready for Chapter Six

6

Here are five vocabulary words that are used in the story about the War of 1812. Study these definitions so you will know what each word means when you see it in your reading.

anthem   (AN-them)   A song which praises a country. "The Star-Spangled Banner" is our national anthem.

coward   (COW-urd)   A person who is easily scared; one who is not brave.

treaty   (TREE-tee)   An agreement which nations sign, often at the end of a war.

pioneer   (py-uh-NEER)   One of the first settlers in a new land.

regiment   (REJ-ih-ment)   A large group of soldiers commanded by a colonel (KER-nel).

The War of 1812

Chapter 6

Why did the United States go to war with England in 1812?
What was unusual about the treaty ending the War of 1812?
What were the results of the war?

> "Oh! say can you see
>   By the dawn's early light . . ."

These are the opening words of "The Star-Spangled Banner." America's *national* **anthem** was written during the War of 1812.

NA-shun-ul

In 1812 France and England were at war. American ships trading with Europe were stopped by the British navy. The British were trying to keep the French from receiving food or supplies.

The British were also capturing American ships at sea. They kidnaped American sailors at gunpoint. England needed men for her navy. She said the Americans she took were British sailors who had run away from the British navy. A few of them were. The captured Americans were *forced* to work on British ships. ●

FORST

Many Americans depended on trade for a living. Trade meant making or growing things here and selling them to other countries. The other countries would sell their goods to us. We would bring them back here to sell. When trade stopped, people lost their jobs. Ships sat empty at their docks, with no place to go. ●

And so the United States stopped being neutral and went to war with England in 1812. The first step was to try to conquer Canada, which was part of the British Empire. General William Hull was ordered to invade Canada from *Detroit*. Instead of fighting, Hull surrendered Detroit to the British without firing a shot. He was sentenced to be shot for being a **coward**, but the order was never carried out.

dee-TROYT

The War of 1812 was full of mistakes by both sides. The British tried to attack the United States from Canada, but were thrown back. Other British forces did *manage* to capture Washington, D.C., our capital, though. President James Madison and his wife, Dolley, escaped from the city just in time. The British then set fire to the White House and other public buildings. They moved on to Baltimore, where they were stopped by a large American army.

MAN-ij

When the British attacked Baltimore, a man named Francis Scott Key was there. He could clearly see the American flag flying over the fort which was defending the city. His heart filled with feeling, Key wrote "The Star-Spangled Banner," our national anthem. Its words begin this chapter. ●

By 1814, both sides were tired of the war. A **treaty** of peace was worked out and *signed* in Europe. The treaty just said that the war was

SYND

to stop. Neither England nor America was the winner. The war ended in a tie.

But the fighting was not really over. News of the treaty took weeks to reach America because there were no telephones or television sets then. A sailing ship brought the news. Meanwhile, one of the greatest battles in American history was fought. ●

The British had sent a large army to capture *New Orleans*, Louisiana. The army was then supposed to march up the Mississippi River and conquer the western United States. The British were very sure of themselves. Their troops had fought and defeated the French in Europe.

noo OR-lee-unz

The Americans put together an army that used **pioneers** from Tennessee and Kentucky and two **regiments** of Blacks from New Orleans. Most of these men were good hunters and tough fighters. The American commander was Andrew Jackson, of Tennessee.

In January 1815, the British attacked New Orleans. In their bright red coats they made perfect targets for the American sharpshooters. Over two thousand British were killed or wounded before the rest ran away. The Americans lost eight men.

That was the end of the strange War of 1812. No one won, no one lost. But the war had one important *result*. Because of the victory at New Orleans, General Andrew Jackson became the greatest American hero since George Washington. Like Washington, Jackson was later elected president.

ree-ZULT

Answer these to review the main ideas.

A.

1. How did "The Star-Spangled Banner" come to be written? _____

_____

2. Why was trade important to the American people? _____

_____

What happened when trade stopped? _____

_____

3. What did the British do with the American sailors they captured?

_____

_____

4. Who won the War of 1812? _____

_____

5. Why didn't the war stop when the peace treaty was signed? _____

_____

_____

6. How did the American people feel about Andrew Jackson after the

war? _____

_____

B.

Circle True or False.

T　F　1. General William Hull was a hero in the War of 1812.

T　F　2. Trade means making goods here to sell to other countries.

T　F　3. The British were unable to capture our capital, Washington, D.C.

T　F　4. The Battle of New Orleans was fought after the peace treaty ending the war was signed.

T　F　5. More Americans than British were killed at the Battle of New Orleans.

C.

Circle the right answer to finish each sentence.

1. "The Star-Spangled Banner" was written by

   a. Thomas Jefferson　b. Francis Scott Key　c. Andrew Jackson

2. "The Star-Spangled Banner" was written during a British attack on

   a. Washington　　　b. Detroit　　　c. Baltimore

3. The man who was president during the War of 1812 was

   a. John Adams　　　b. James Madison　　c. Thomas Jefferson

4. The British wanted to keep food and supplies from reaching

   a. Spain　　　　b. the United States　c. France

5. Andrew Jackson's home was in

   a. Massachusetts　b. Tennessee　　　c. Connecticut

Choose one of these words to fit each sentence below.

regiment   pioneer   coward   anthem   treaty

1. A person who gets frightened easily and runs away from things that frighten him or her is a _____.

2. "The Star-Spangled Banner" is our national _____.

3. A person who moves into new or unsettled lands is a

   _____.

4. A colonel commands a _____ of soldiers.

5. At the end of a war, nations sign an agreement called a

   _____.

Think about and discuss in class.

Do you think the British had a right to stop American ships going to

Europe? _____ What else could they have done? _____

_____

_____

Can a person be afraid of something and still not be a coward? _____

Are heroes ever afraid? Give examples. _____

_____

_____

Would you like to be a pioneer? _____ Where could you

go? _____

_____

Andrew Jackson was a hero of the American people. Who are some of your heroes or heroines today? Can people be heroes and heroines without

being soldiers? _____

_____

_____

_____

D.

E.

HEH-row-inz

Father Hidalgo was a Mexican priest who called on the Mexican people to fight for freedom from Spain.

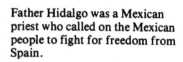

Monroe did not want European armies to move into the Americas. In return, he promised that the United States would not meddle in Europe's affairs.

President James Monroe told his cabinet it was time to tell Europe not to start any more colonies in North or South America.

Getting Ready for Chapter Seven

7

Here are five vocabulary words that are used in the story about Spain's colonies and the Monroe Doctrine. Study these definitions so you will know what each word means when you see it in your reading.

empire   (EM-pire) A group of colonies run by a single government. The American colonies were part of the British Empire.

rejoice   (ree-JOYSS) To be very glad about something.

patriot   (PAY-tree-ot) A person who deeply loves his or her country.

sympathy   (SIM-puh-thee) Caring about and understanding someone's feelings.

doctrine   (DOK-trin) A statement which says what a country believes and thinks should be done about something.

Hands Off the Americas!

There was a new spirit of freedom in the world in the early 1800s.
How did the Monroe Doctrine protect new nations?
How did it show the strength of America?

Viva la Independencia! In English, these Spanish words mean "Long live independence!" They were spoken by a Mexican priest, Father *Hidalgo*, in 1810. Father Hidalgo called on the Mexican people to follow him in a fight for freedom from Spain.

VEE-vah-lah
een-day-payn-DAYN-tsee-a
ee-DAHL-gow

For over three hundred years Spain had ruled a rich **empire** in North America and South America. But Spain grew weak from its wars with England and France. Mexico and South America thought this was a good time to try to get rid of harsh Spanish rule.

When the United States won independence from England, Mexicans **rejoiced**. They wanted to do the same thing. They, too, rebelled and fought for freedom. But Father Hidalgo came to a sad end. The Spaniards captured him and killed him. Then they carried his head through the streets in an iron cage. This was a warning to the Mexicans to stop their revolution. ●

People still kept working for revolution — in Mexico and all over. A **patriot** named *Simon Bolivar* got together an army that won freedom for Colombia, *Venezuela*, and Peru. Bolivar is called "the George Washington of South America." Other generals defeated Spanish forces in *Chile* and *Argentina*. By 1823, almost all Spanish colonies from Mexico to the tip of South America were free. At the same time, Brazil won independence from Portugal.

SEE-mown BOW-lee-var
ve-nez-WAY-luh

CHIH-lee
ar-jen-TEE-nuh

Other European nations worried about Spain's defeats. The new spirit of freedom in the world was a threat to countries which had colonies.

France, Russia, and other European countries offered to help Spain get her colonies back. Russia, like the United States, claimed the Oregon country and warned other nations to stay out of that area. ●

James Monroe was president of the United States at this time. Monroe had fought beside George Washington in the American Revolution. He had been *wounded* in the chest and he still felt the pain. The president had strong feelings of **sympathy** for anyone willing to fight for freedom.

WOON-did

Monroe did not want European armies to move into Oregon, Mexico, and South America. He was afraid they might attack the United States, too. He also wanted Oregon for the United States.

After talking things over with his cabinet, Monroe decided what to do. The United States was still young, but it was getting stronger. It was time to show the world that it was not afraid of anybody. Europe could take care of its own side of the Atlantic Ocean. The United States would protect North and South America.

In 1823 President Monroe announced the Monroe **Doctrine**. He made three things clear to the rulers of Europe. First, he warned them not to start any more colonies in North and South America. Second, he told them not to attack any of the countries that had just won freedom from Spain. Third, Monroe promised that the United States would not meddle in Europe's affairs.

Coming from a small young nation, this was tough talk. We had fought for our own freedom from England. Now we were saying that we would not let anyone attack the freedom of our *neighbors*.

NAY-burz

The British supported the Monroe Doctrine. England, our old enemy, became our friend. She offered to help us with her powerful navy if anyone attacked Spain's former colonies. No one dared to, because the United States and England together were too strong.

The Monroe Doctrine played an important part in American history. It protected our Latin American neighbors from Spain and her allies. It kept the Russians from Oregon. It told the world that the United States would stand up and fight for freedom everywhere in the Americas.

Answer these to review the main ideas.

A.

1. Why did Europe's rulers want to help Spain get back her colonies?

_____

_____

2. Why did President James Monroe feel sympathy for people who were willing to fight for freedom? _____

_____

3. Why didn't President Monroe want foreign armies to attack the Oregon country and Latin America? _____

_____

4. What were the three points that the president made in his Monroe

   Doctrine? _____

   _____

   _____

Circle True or False.   B.

T F 1. Father Hidalgo was captured and killed by Spanish
          soldiers.

T F 2. England believed in the Monroe Doctrine and offered to
          help the United States.

T F 3. President Monroe had been wounded in the War of 1812.

T F 4. President Monroe declared that the United States had the
          right to meddle in Europe's affairs.

T F 5. The United States wanted to keep other countries out of the
          Americas.

Circle the right answer to finish each sentence.   C.

1. The "George Washington of South America" was

   a. James Monroe   b. Simon Bolivar   c. Father Hidalgo

2. Brazil won its independence from

   a. Portugal   b. the United States   c. Spain

3. The Russians warned the rest of the world to stay out of

   a. New Mexico   b. Louisiana   c. Oregon

4. The Monroe Doctrine was announced in

   a. 1812   b. 1815   c. 1823

5. "Viva la Independencia!" means

   a. Forget about   b. You can depend   c. Long live
      independence!   upon it!   independence!

Choose one of these words to fit each sentence below.   D.

   empire   rejoice   patriot   sympathy   doctrine

1. James Monroe gave his name to the Monroe _____.

2. Monroe had feelings of _____ for countries that were

willing to fight for freedom.

3. A group of colonies run by one strong government is an

_____.

4. A person who loves his or her country very much is a

_____.

5. To be very happy and glad about something is to _____.

Think about and discuss in class.

Can you think of any Latin American countries that still belonged to

Spain after 1823? Hint: Think about countries on islands. _____

_____

Do you think we still pay attention to the Monroe Doctrine? Ask your

parents or teacher what they think. _____

_____

_____

_____

E.

Jackson ordered thousands of
Native Americans living in the
East to move west of the
Mississippi River because
white men wanted their land.
Many of them died on the
long, hard trip, which was
called the Trail of Tears.

Jackson fought against Native Americans when they were on the British side in the War of 1812.

Getting Ready for Chapter Eight

8

Here are six vocabulary words that are used in the story about Andrew Jackson. Study these definitions so you will know what each word means when you see it in your reading.

boldly   (BOWLD-lee) Bravely, showing daring and courage.

orphan   (OR-fun)   A young person whose parents are dead.

hickory   (HICK-ur-ee)   A kind of tree with hard, tough wood.

inaugurate   (in-AW-gyoor-ayt)   To swear into office. (Usually said of presidents.)

protest   (prow-TEST)   To disagree strongly. To speak out against something.

deserve   (duh-ZURV)   To earn or to be entitled to something.

Andrew Jackson, Man of the People

What kind of a man was Andrew Jackson?
Do you think he was a good president? Why or why not?

Our first six American presidents came from just two states — Massachusetts and Virginia. They were easterners, who were mostly rich and well *educated*. Even Thomas Jefferson, who said he liked the plain people, lived very well in a *beautiful* home. He also owned slaves.

EH-joo-kay-tid
BYOO-ti-full

The first president who came from the plain, common people themselves was Andrew Jackson. As you have read, Jackson was the hero of the Battle of New Orleans in the War of 1812.

Jackson was born somewhere along the frontier of the two Carolinas in 1767. When he was only thirteen he fought against the British when they invaded the Carolinas during the American Revolution. Jackson was captured and ordered to shine a British officer's boots. But he was very brave and stubborn, and he refused. In a fit of anger, the British officer slashed Jackson across the face with his sword. The scar—and his hatred of the British—lasted for the rest of Jackson's life.

Jackson's mother and father died at a young age. The boy was an **orphan** when he was fourteen. He studied law and went west to make his home in Tennessee. Jackson was strong and tough. He killed one man in a *duel* and was almost killed in another. When Native Americans sided with the British in the War of 1812, he fought against them. •

DOO-ul

In 1818, Spain still owned Florida, but the Spanish government was weak. The Spaniards could not stop the fighting between the Native Americans and the white settlers who lived along the borders. Jackson **boldly** led an army into Florida and claimed the land for the United States. Spain did not dare to challenge him and sold us Florida in the next year (1819).

For being so *rough* and daring, Jackson was given a nickname. Somebody said he was as tough as **hickory** wood. From then on, he was known as "Old Hickory." •

RUFF

Jackson was elected president in 1828. He was the first president to come from a western state. Tennessee was on the western frontier in those days. The people in the West were very proud of Jackson.

Thousands of Jackson's followers went to Washington to *celebrate* his election. After he was **inaugurated**, a big party was held at the White House. Many people went. There was so much excitement that windows were broken and furniture was turned over.

SEL-eh-brayt

"Old Hickory" was president for two terms. He paid attention to the wishes of the people who had elected him. Alexander Hamilton had started a government bank called the Bank of the United States. Rich people managed the bank and *controlled* the country's money supply. Jackson didn't think this was fair. He ordered the bank closed. He set up a different system of state banks, but they were not as safe as the Bank of the United States. His enemies then gave him another nickname. They called him "King Andrew the First" because he did as he pleased. ●

While Jackson was president, South Carolina **protested** against a tax law that Congress had passed. The people in that state said they would not obey the law. Jackson acted quickly, as he usually did. He told South Carolina to obey the law. If it did not, he said he would send an army of 50,000 there to make people obey it. Soon there was an agreement with South Carolina. Congress lowered the tax, and South Carolina agreed to pay it. ●

Many people think that Jackson was not fair to Native Americans. He ordered thousands of these people living in the East to be moved west of the Mississippi River to Oklahoma. They had done nothing to **deserve** such treatment. They were sent away just because white men wanted their land. Many Native Americans died on the long trip. They called it the "Trail of Tears."

There were good things as well as bad about Andrew Jackson. But his manners were like those of the plain American people. He felt as they did. He hated and loved the same things that they did. The American people elected Jackson, and Jackson spoke for them.

kun-TROWLD

Answer these to review the main ideas.

A.

1. How was Andrew Jackson different from the presidents before

   him? _____

   _____

2. What troubles did Jackson have in the early years of his life? _____

   _____

3. How did Jackson get the name "Old Hickory?" _____

   _____

4. How did Jackson treat Native Americans?_____

   _____

Circle the right answer to finish each sentence.

B.

1. Andrew Jackson was born

    a. on the frontier   b. in Florida   c. in New York

2. Jackson was so tough that he was called

    a. Andrew the Great   b. Old Hickory   c. Old Rough and Ready

3. In 1828 Tennessee was

    a. a northern state   b. an eastern state   c. a western state

4. Jackson was president for

    a. one term   b. two terms   c. three terms

5. The Bank of the United States was run by

    a. rich people   b. poor people   c. plain people

What happened on each of the following dates?

C.

1. 1767 _____

2. 1818 _____

3. 1819 _____

4. 1828 _____

Circle True or False.

D.

T F 1. Our first six presidents all came from western states.

T F 2. Andrew Jackson hated the British and Native Americans.

T F 3. Many Native Americans had to leave their land in the East because the white men wanted it.

T F 4. Jackson threatened to send 50,000 soldiers to South Carolina to make the people there obey the law.

T F 5. Jackson thought the Bank of the United States was good for the country because it was run by smart people.

Choose one of these words to fit each sentence below.

E.

boldly   orphan   hickory

inaugurate   protest   deserve

1. A child whose parents are not living is an _____.

2. People who do kind things _____ to do well.

3. When will our next president be _____ d?

4. When other people were wondering what to do, Jackson acted

_____.

5. Andrew Jackson was so tough that he was called "Old

_____.''

6. Sometimes if we are badly treated we _____ against it.

Think about and discuss in class.

Was Jackson a strong or a weak leader? _____ Would

you have been glad to have him as your president? Explain. _____

_____

_____

How can a leader tell what the wishes of the people are? _____

_____

Can you think of a time when he or she should act against them? _____

_____

Who do you think would make a better president, one of the plain
people with little money, or someone successful in business with a lot

of money? _____

_____

Can a person who does not have much money become president now?

_____

_____

Machines and electricity changed American life. Children worked long hours in factories for very little pay. They often had no time to go to school.

The South was using more and more slaves to pick cotton. People were beginning to argue about whether a free country should allow slavery.

Steam engines were used on ships to turn the large paddle wheels. The engines made these ships move much faster than sails could.

9

Getting Ready for Chapter Nine

Here are five vocabulary words that are used in the story about changes in American life. Study these definitions so you will know what each word means when you see it in your reading.

freight	(FRAYT)	Things carried from one place to another on a train, boat, or plane.
produce	(pruh-DOOS)	To make.
cause	(KOZ)	To make something happen.
wages	(WAY-juz)	Amount of money paid for work.
reform	(ree-FORM)	Changing of something to make it better; improvement.

Changes in American Life

How did life change for Americans in the 1800s?
Was it better for everybody?
Who were the reformers? How did they want to improve
our country?

Chapter 9

Before the 1800s people had almost no *machines* to help them. They walked or rode horses to get places. They made by hand their own clothes, *furniture*, and other things they used. Then life in America changed. New *inventions* changed people's lives.

About two hundred years ago in England the steam *engine* was invented. Wood and coal made these engines go. They were put on ships which had large paddle wheels. When the engines ran, they turned the paddle wheels. This made the ships move at a faster speed than sailing ships. Robert Fulton, an American, built the first *successful* steamboat in 1807.

Steamships were better than sailing ships in another way. Steamships could move ahead in all kinds of weather. Sailing ships had to depend on just the right wind. If it blew too hard or not at all, the sailing ships could not go.

One invention led to another. Steam engines were placed on wheels that ran on railroad tracks. The engines pulled train cars behind them. These trains could travel much faster than horses. They carried both people and **freight**. ●

Machines changed life on the farm, too. In 1793 *Eli Whitney* invented the cotton gin (engine). It took the seeds out of cotton much faster than slaves could do it by hand. Farmers planted more cotton and bought more slaves to pick it. Slavery spread all across the South and Southwest.

In the 1840s, inventors learned how to use electricity. Samuel F. B. Morse built the first telegraph in 1837. Messages could be sent on wires across the country in a matter of seconds.

Machines and electricity changed American life. People worked at machines in factories. They **produced** clothes, furniture, pots and pans, and hundreds of other things that families used to make at home. These goods were made much faster and more cheaply by machines than they had been by hand.

The factory workers lived near the places where they worked. Cities grew up around the factories. Fast-moving trains connected the cities. ●

All these changes made life easier for some people. They enjoyed the new goods that had been invented. But the new times also **caused** problems. Women and children worked in the factories for six days a week from dawn until dark. Factory owners paid their workers low **wages.** Those who were paid little could not buy many of the good things of life.

In the South, slavery was becoming very important. More and more slaves were needed to work in the cotton fields. Factory owners in the North bought all the cotton the South could send them. ●

Some Americans worried about the changes in the way people lived. Churchmen and plain citizens demanded **reforms.** They wanted life to be better for everybody, not just a few. In the 1830s, factory workers asked for shorter hours and more pay. They also said it was *cruel* to make children work long hours six days a week.

KROO-ul

Women were angry, too. They could not vote or own property. Elizabeth Cady Stanton and Susan B. Anthony led the fight to get women equal rights with men.

The biggest battle of all was over slavery. The South was growing quickly. More and more slaves were needed to do work cheaply. Some people felt strongly that slavery had no place in a country where people were supposed to be free and equal.

Southerners defended slavery. They said their slaves were happier than Northern children working in factories. The arguing went on. As America grew, it was also starting to split apart over the problem of slavery.

Answer these to review the main ideas.

A.

1. How did the invention of the steam engine change the way people

   traveled? _____

   _____

2. What happened to slavery when the cotton gin was invented? _____

   _____

3. What kind of reforms did Americans demand in the early 1800s?

   _____

   _____

4. What were the arguments *for* slavery? _____

   _____

Circle the right answer to finish each sentence.

B.

1. Before the age of machines Americans traveled by

   a. trolley car　　　b. airplane　　　c. foot, horseback, or sail

2. Robert Fulton built the first successful steamboat in

   a. 1807　　　b. 1776　　　c. 1800

3. Eli Whitney's cotton gin was able to

   a. plant cotton　　　b. remove the seeds from cotton　　　c. harvest cotton

4. The first telegraph was built by

   a. Robert Fulton　　　b. Samuel F. B. Morse　　　c. Eli Whitney

Circle True or False.

C.

T　F　1. Fewer slaves were needed after Eli Whitney invented the cotton gin.

T　F　2. The steam engine was invented in the United States.

T　F　3. It took weeks to send a telegraph message across the country.

T　F　4. Women and children had to work in factories from dawn until dark six days a week.

T　F　5. Southerners said that their slaves were better off than the women and children who worked in Northern factories.

Draw a line from the person in the first column to what he or she did in the second column.

D.

Eli Whitney　　　　　　Built first successful steamboat

Elizabeth Cady Stanton　　Invented the telegraph

Samuel F. B. Morse　　　Fought for women's rights

Robert Fulton　　　　　Invented the cotton gin

Susan B. Anthony

Choose one of these words to fit each sentence below.

freight   produce   cause   wages   reform

1. People get _____ in return for their work.

2. Trains carry people and _____ from one part of the country to another.

3. Factories were able to _____ things faster than people working at home could.

4. Slavery _____ d serious problems for this country.

5. Because people were unhappy with the changes in their way of life they demanded _____ .

Think about and discuss in class.

With your teacher's help, find out what you can about the following women reformers — then discuss them in class: Elizabeth Cady Stanton, Susan B. Anthony, Dorothea Dix. _____

_____

_____

Some people blame the invention of the cotton gin for the growth of slavery in the South. Do you agree with this argument? _____ Explain. _____

_____

_____

Do women have equal rights with men now? _____

_____

What reforms would you like to see made in our country today? _____

_____

_____

_____

E.

F.

In the war to make Texas independent, Americans fought a long, hard battle against Mexicans at the Alamo. They lost after eleven days of fighting. Every Texan was killed.

Davy Crockett was a frontier hero from Tennessee who was killed in the battle at the Alamo.

Santa Anna, the Mexican general, was captured in a surprise attack by Sam Houston's men. Santa Anna surrendered, and Texas was free.

Getting Ready for Chapter Ten

10

Here are seven vocabulary words that are used in the story about Texas. Study these definitions so you will know what each word means when you see it in your reading.

fertile   (FUR-til)   Rich in material which is good for plants and helps them grow.

contract   (KON-trakt)   A written agreement.

gringo   (GRIN-gow)   Latin-American word for foreigners, especially Americans.

customs   (KUSS-tumz)   Habits. The way people do things. (Drinking tea is an English custom.)

immigrant   (IM-ih-grunt)   A person who leaves one country to settle in another.

dictator   (DIK-tay-tur)   A ruler who has complete control of the government. What he says is the law.

republic   (ree-PUH-blik)   Any government headed by a president instead of a king or queen.

Texas, the Lone Star State

Why did Americans settle in Texas?
How did Texas win its freedom?
What happened to the Republic of Texas?

In 1821 Mexico won freedom from Spain. Mexicans were proud of their large, new country. It included Mexico and a great deal more — Texas, Arizona, New Mexico, Nevada, *Utah*, and California. All of this land had belonged to Spain.

YOO-toh

Although California and the Southwest were large, not many settlers lived there. The forts and missions founded by Father Serra and other Spaniards were still there, and several Native American nations lived off the land. The settlers wanted to take over the thousands of miles of **fertile** land and farm it. •

At this time large numbers of Americans were moving west in search of new land. One of them, Stephen Austin, had inherited from his father a **contract** with the Mexican government. In the contract, Austin agreed to bring three hundred American families to Texas in return for land there. The Americans would raise cotton and cattle. Austin would own the land. Since Texas belonged to Mexico, the Americans would have to obey Mexican laws.

At first the Mexicans welcomed the **gringos**, as they called the Americans. They were glad to see land being used. But soon foreigners were *pouring* in by the thousands. Most of the gringos were Southerners, who brought along their slaves.

POR-ing

Too late, Mexico realized it had made a mistake. Texas was a very big place. In 1835, there were about twenty thousand settlers and four thousand slaves in Texas. Only three or four thousand Mexicans lived there. The Americans did not want to learn Mexican ways. They had their own language, religion, and **customs**.

The Mexican government said there could be no more slavery in Texas. It also refused to take in any more American **immigrants**. The Americans in Texas paid no attention to these laws. In 1836 they declared independence from Mexico. But Mexico did not want to give up Texas. •

Mexico's president was a **dictator** and soldier named Santa Anna. General Santa Anna led an army into Texas. The Americans were waiting for him at San Antonio. They had made an old mission building into a fort called the *Alamo*. It had high walls all around it.

A-luh-mow

General Santa Anna had about three thousand men in his army. The Texans had fewer than two hundred, but they were *tough* frontiersmen. When the Mexicans attacked the fort, the Texans drove them back.

TUFF

Santa Anna was furious. He warned the Texans to surrender at once, or his men would kill them all. Colonel William Travis of the Texans replied, "I shall never surrender or retreat."

It took the Mexicans eleven days to capture the Alamo. The Texans fought to the last man. Not one of them came out alive. Among the dead was Davy Crockett, a frontier hero from Tennessee.

General Santa Anna kept fighting. At *Goliad* his troops killed three hundred Texans. The war was going well for the Mexicans.

GOW-lee-ad

The Texan army was commanded by Sam Houston of Tennessee. Houston had served with Andrew Jackson in the War of 1812. The two men were good friends and were very much alike. They were tough pioneers and soldiers.

Houston's small army surprised Santa Anna at *San Jacinto*. The Texans were hidden in the woods when the Mexicans came by. Shouting "Remember the Alamo!" Houston's men opened fire. Then they charged. Santa Anna's army was destroyed, and the Mexican general was captured. Houston made Santa Anna sign a paper of surrender. ●

san huh-SEEN-tow

Texas had won its freedom from Mexico. The Texan flag had just one single star, and the country was called the Lone Star **Republic**. A few months later, Sam Houston became the first president of Texas. But the Texans did not want to remain an independent nation. They were Americans, and they wanted to be part of the United States. They asked to become another one of our country's states.

Nine years went by before Texas became a part of the United States. Americans had many arguments about it. Northerners said that Texas had slaves. They said the spread of slavery must be stopped. Another problem was that Mexico still claimed that Texas belonged to her. Mexico *threatened* to go to war if the United States took over Texas.

THREH-tend

Our southern and western states finally had their way in 1845. Congress invited Texas to join the United States. The Texans quickly accepted the invitation. The Lone Star Republic then became the Lone Star State.

Answer these to review the main ideas.

A.

1. After Mexico won freedom from Spain, what western parts of the United States did it include? _____

_____

2. What was the agreement between Stephen Austin and the Mexican government? _____

_____

3. Why did Texas declare independence from Mexico? _____

_____

4. What happened at the Alamo? _____

_____

5. What happened at the Battle of San Jacinto? _____

_____

6. Why did Americans argue so long over letting Texas join the United States? _____

_____

Circle the right answer to finish each sentence.

B.

1. Mexico won its independence from Spain in

   a. 1776   b. 1821   c. 1814

2. The man who agreed to bring Americans to Texas was

   a. Santa Anna   b. Stephen Austin   c. Andrew Jackson

3. The fort at San Antonio where the Texans fought to the last man was called

   a. the Alamo   b. Goliad   c. San Jacinto

4. A *gringo* is

   a. a Spaniard   b. an Indian   c. an American

5. The Texan army was commanded by

   a. Davy Crockett   b. Santa Anna   c. Sam Houston

Circle True or False.

C.

T   F   1. Mexico once owned California, Texas, New Mexico, Arizona, Utah, and Nevada.

T   F   2. Mexico agreed that Americans in Texas could make their own laws.

T   F   3. Most Americans who went to Texas were Northerners.

T   F   4. The Americans in Texas wanted to learn Mexican ways of living.

T   F   5. No American slaves were brought into Texas.

Choose one of these words to fit each sentence below.

D.

fertile   contract   gringo
customs   immigrant   dictator
republic

1. A written agreement is a _____.

2. A ruler who runs the government without letting the people have any say is a _____.

3. A foreigner who comes to live in America is an _____.

4. Rich soil that produces healthy plants is _____.

5. A country that has a president is a _____.

6. To Latin Americans, an American is a _____.

7. _____ are often different in different parts of the world.

Think about and discuss in class.

E.

Why didn't the Mexicans and the Americans from Texas get along better? _____

_____

Whose fault was it that they went to war? _____

_____

Research the Battle of the Alamo; then role-play it, taking one side or the other. _____

_____

Have you ever heard of Davy Crockett? _____ See what you can find out about this famous Western hero. _____

_____

_____

The United States is a republic. China and Russia are also republics. Is there any difference between a democracy and a republic? _____

_____

_____

When Mexico refused to sell California, war started. The United States was a big, rich country, but Mexico was small and poor. Mexico surrendered in 1848. She lost California and other Western lands (see map).

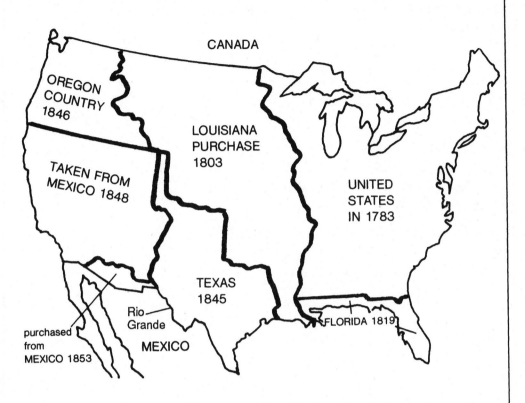

GROWTH OF THE UNITED STATES TO 1853

Because we won the Mexican War, we gained enough land in the West to make the United States stretch from coast to coast.

Getting Ready for Chapter Eleven

11

Here are four vocabulary words that are used in the story about how America came to reach from coast to coast. Study these definitions so you will know what each word means when you see it in your reading.

shrewd   (SHROOD)   Clever and sharp.

accuse   (uh-KYOOZ)   To charge someone with doing something wrong.

cadet   (ka-DETT)   A person studying at a military school to become an officer.

bully   (BULL-lee)   Someone who picks on people who are smaller or weaker.

America Reaches from Coast to Coast

How did President Polk handle the problem of Oregon?
What did Mexico lose in the Mexican war?

President Santa Anna of Mexico was upset at his country's defeat by Texas. He still claimed that Texas belonged to Mexico. He was ready to fight for Texas all over again.

Up north in the United States, the Americans had a new president. He was James K. *Polk* of Tennessee. Like other Americans, Polk wanted to see his country grow. He wanted the United States to stretch from the Atlantic coast to the Pacific coast.

POWLK

American pioneers were pushing west of the Rocky Mountains into the Oregon country. The Oregon country reached all the way from Alaska south to California. The British also claimed it. British pioneers lived there. It looked as if America and England would go to war over Oregon. ●

Other Americans moved into California, which belonged to Mexico. They wrote home about California's rich land and sunshine. They said it should become part of the United States.

President Polk could not stop our people from moving into land belonging to Mexico. The Mexican government treated Americans well, but did not want to give up California. Polk made an *effort* to avoid war. He offered to buy California and the Southwest from Mexico. He was willing to pay a high price — forty million dollars. But the proud Mexicans refused. Instead, they demanded that the United States return Texas to them.

EF-urt

Polk now realized that we would soon be at war with Mexico. He did not want to fight England over Oregon while he was fighting Mexico. Two wars at once would be too much to handle. So Polk made a **shrewd** bargain with England. America and England divided up the Oregon country and became friends again. ●

Now Polk was free to deal with Mexico, which still would not sell California. In 1846 he sent an army to the *Rio Grande*, a river on the Mexican border. General *Zachary* Taylor led the American forces. The Mexicans rushed troops there, too, and fighting began. Each side **accused** the other of starting the war.

ree-ow GRAHND-ay
ZAK-uh-ree

The United States was a large, rich nation. Mexico was poor, and really no match for the Americans. It was a short but hard war.

The Americans who were living in California revolted against

Mexico, the way they had in Texas. Under John C. Fremont, they started their own country, the "Bear Flag Republic." When American soldiers arrived in California, the Bear Flag came down. In its place went the American flag, the Stars and Stripes.

Finally, General Winfield Scott led the American attack on Mexico City, the enemy's capital city. Young **cadets** from Mexico's national military school stood in their way. The boys died fighting to the end, just as the Americans at the Alamo had. Mexico surrendered in 1848, and the fighting stopped. General Santa Anna had lost another war.

Some of our own people, *especially* Northerners, were strongly against the Mexican War. They said that we were big **bullies** trying to push Mexico around. Worse yet, they thought that we were wrong and Mexico was right. They thought we were trying to conquer Mexico in order to bring slavery to the Southwest and California. ●

es-PESH-ul-ee

Because of the Mexican War, the United States became a big power. The country stretched from coast to coast. In the west, it included Washington, Oregon, and California. In the Southwest, the United States owned Arizona, New Mexico, and Texas. Other states taken from Mexico were Nevada, Utah, and parts of Colorado and Wyoming. For her loss of western lands, Mexico was paid fifteen million dollars by the United States. Americans thought the price was fair. Mexicans did not.

President James Polk is not often thought of as an American hero. He was a quiet man who didn't say much and who worked hard. Polk worked so hard, in fact, that he died a few weeks after leaving the White House. What he did was important. The whole western part of our country, from the Rocky Mountains to the Pacific coast, became part of the United States.

Answer these to review the main ideas.

A.

1. How did President Santa Anna of Mexico feel about losing Texas?

_____

2. How did President Polk try to avoid war with Mexico? _____

_____

3. How did President Polk avoid getting into two wars at the same

time? _____

_____

4. Why were some Americans against fighting Mexico? _____

_____

5. What land did the United States gain from the Mexican War?

_____

Circle the right answer to finish each sentence.   **B.**

1. When Mexico refused to sell California, President Polk sent troops to

   a. the Mississippi   b. the Hudson River   c. the Rio Grande
      River

2. The Oregon country stretched all the way from Alaska south to

   a. Canada   b. California   c. Arizona

3. For the land she took from Mexico, the United States paid

   a. one million   b. fifty million   c. fifteen million
      dollars   dollars   dollars

4. The Mexican War began in

   a. 1846   b. 1826   c. 1860

Circle True or False.   **C.**

T   F   1. President Santa Anna said that Texas still belonged to
           Mexico.

T   F   2. Americans in California said that it was not a good place to
           live.

T   F   3. England refused to divide the Oregon country with the
           United States.

T   F   4. Americans everywhere were strongly in favor of war with
           Mexico.

T   F   5. The Americans living in California remained loyal to
           Mexico.

Choose one of these words to fit each sentence below.   **D.**

   bully   shrewd   accuse   cadet

1. A person who goes to a military school, such as West Point, is a

_____ .

2. Do not _____ that man of being a thief.

3. President Polk was _____ when he made a bargain with England.

4. A person who picks a fight with a smaller, weaker person is a

_____.

Think about and discuss in class.

E.

Why isn't James K. Polk an American hero like George Washington

or Andrew Jackson? _____

_____

What makes a good soldier? Is courage alone enough? How important

are training and good weapons? _____

_____

Was James K. Polk a good leader? Did he bully Mexico? Or was he simply doing his duty, carrying out the wishes of the American

people? _____

_____

_____

_____

Gold was discovered in 1848 in a river at Sutter's Mill in California.

The forty-niners hoped to become rich, but most of them did not find gold.

People hoping to find gold made the long, hard trip to California. The cheapest and most popular way to go was by covered wagon. It took several months to get there.

Getting Ready for Chapter Twelve

12

Here are five vocabulary words that are used in the story about gold in California. Study these definitions so you will know what each word means when you see it in your reading.

outpost	(OUT-powst) A settlement away from the main body of troops. It has a fort where soldiers watch for the enemy.
blacksmith	(BLAK-smith) A person who melts iron and makes it into horseshoes or tools.
sawmill	(SAW-mil) A place where logs are sawn into boards and planks.
mobile	(MOW-bil) Easy to move.
prairie	(PRAIR-ee) Flat or slightly rolling land covered with grass, but few trees.

Gold in California

Who was John Sutter?
What was the secret between Sutter and James Marshall?
What happened when the secret leaked out?

John Sutter came to America from Switzerland to find a better life. After traveling around the country, he arrived in California in 1839. At that time, California still belonged to Mexico.

The Mexican governor in California gave Sutter a very large ranch near Sacramento. Sutter agreed to make it into an **outpost** against the Russians in Alaska. After a while he built a fort, a lumber mill, a **blacksmith** shop, and several small factories. He raised cattle, horses, and sheep.

Sutter was very hard-working. He brought hundreds of people to work on his ranch. Native Americans worked hard in the wheat fields. Skilled workers from the United States ran the mills and factories. Sutter lived in a building like a *castle* and acted like a king.

KASS-ul

In 1846 the Mexican War began. California was taken over by the United States. American soldiers settled in at Sutter's fort. ●

Then one day in 1848, a carpenter named James Marshall came to Sutter's office. He had been building a **sawmill** for Sutter on the American River. Marshall was *nervous* and excited. "Captain Sutter!" he said. "I have something to show you. But please lock the door first."

NER-vus

Sutter was puzzled, but he locked the door. Marshall shook some yellow pebbles and dust out of a rag into his hand. Sutter stared at the pebbles. "Looks like gold," he said.

"It *is* gold!" Marshall exclaimed. "I found it in the river on your property, Captain Sutter. There's lots of it! You're rich! There are millions and billions of dollars worth of gold in the river!"

Sutter and Marshall tested the pebbles. There was no *doubt* of it. The pebbles were pure gold.

DOUT

"We'll keep this a secret between us," Sutter told Marshall. "Meanwhile, I want to make sure that my claim to the land is good. I got it from the Mexicans, you know. But now the land belongs to the United States."

Sutter sent a messenger to the American governor at Monterey. The governor replied that it would take a while to find out whether Sutter's land still belonged to him. That was the beginning of the end for the rancher.

Within a few days, news of the discovery of gold leaked out. Someone went to San Francisco with fists full of pebbles, yelling "Gold! Gold in the American River!" People saw — and believed. They started running toward Sutter's property to try to find gold and share some of the riches.

There was no way Sutter could keep the gold hunters out. The courts said that since the United States now controlled California, he no longer owned the land. The visitors dug up his ranch and killed his cattle. For the rest of his life, John Sutter was a poor man. He drowned in a sea of gold. ●

From California, news of the "gold rush" reached Chicago, New York, and New Orleans. For a while it looked as if all the people on the east coast were moving to the west coast. The gold hunters were called the "forty-niners" because they went west in 1849.

In those days there were three ways to get to California from the East. You could go by water around the tip of South America, then north to California on the Pacific Ocean. This took five months. Or you could sail to Mexico or Panama, cross by land, and sail again on the Pacific to San Francisco. This took about five weeks. But it was expensive and dangerous. Many people died of *disease* in the swamps of Panama.

dih-ZEEZ

By far the cheapest and most popular way to go was by covered wagon. Trains and steamboats went as far west as St. Joseph, Missouri. Then travelers changed to covered wagons pulled by mules and oxen. These wagons were the trailers or **mobile** homes of the 1800s. Whole families lived in the wagons. They had all their things with them — stoves, pots and pans, food, furniture, and guns.

The trip from Missouri by covered wagon was two thousand miles across **prairies**, deserts, and mountains. It took several months. Summers were very hot, and water was scarce. Sometimes there were deadly attacks from Native Americans protecting their land. But the worst danger of all came near the end of the trip. Then the pioneers had to cross the mountains called the *Sierra Nevadas*. Heavy snows began falling there in September. Many wagons were caught in the snow, and the pioneers would starve or freeze to death. But the wagons kept coming, slowly crossing Oregon and California on trails to Sutter's fort. ●

see-EH-ruh neh-VAH-duz

In 1848 the population of California was 6,000. In 1849 it rose to 85,000. Some people found gold, and others didn't. But there were jobs for everyone in the fast-growing cities and towns.

Without the gold rush, California might not have become a state for many years. But the gold rush changed history. It made events move faster. In 1850, only two years after Jim Marshall found gold, California became our thirty-first state.

Answer these to review the main ideas.

A.

1. Why did the Mexican governor give John Sutter a large ranch in California? _____

2. How did Sutter lose his claim to the land given to him? _____

_____

3. What finally happened to Sutter and his ranch? _____

_____

4. What were the three ways of going to California from the East?

_____

_____

5. What were some of the dangers of the trip to California? _____

_____

_____

6. How did the gold rush change California? _____

_____

Circle True or False.

B.

T F 1. John Sutter got his land from friends.

T F 2. Sutter had a small ranch with very few laborers on it.

T F 3. Marshall found gold in the Rio Grande.

T F 4. It took three years to get to California from the eastern states.

T F 5. California became our thirty-first state in 1850.

T F 6. Everybody who went to California found gold.

Circle the right answer to finish each sentence.

C.

1. John Sutter came to America from

   a. England   b. Canada   c. Switzerland

2. The Mexican governor gave Sutter a large ranch near

   a. Sacramento   b. San Francisco   c. Los Angeles

3. James Marshall discovered gold in California in

   a. 1846   b. 1848   c. 1850

4. Snow began falling in the Sierra Nevadas in

   a. September   b. November   c. January

5. By 1849, the population of California had risen to

   a. one million   b. one thousand   c. eighty-five
                                         thousand

D. Choose one of these words to fit each sentence below.

blacksmith   prairie   sawmill
mobile   outpost

1. Years ago, horseshoes were made by a _____.

2. The United States has army _____s in other countries.

3. Between the Mississippi River and the Rocky Mountains lie grass-
   lands called _____s.

4. Millions of Americans today live in _____ homes.

5. Tree trunks are brought to _____s to be cut into
   boards and planks.

E. Think about and discuss in class.

The story says that John Sutter "drowned in a sea of gold." Can you

explain this statement? _____

_____

_____

How do you think Native Americans felt about the pioneers? _____

_____

_____

Do you think John Sutter was treated fairly by the Americans? Explain

your answer. _____

_____

_____

Slaves did much of the hard work in the South. Many were treated very badly by their owners. None of them could go to school.

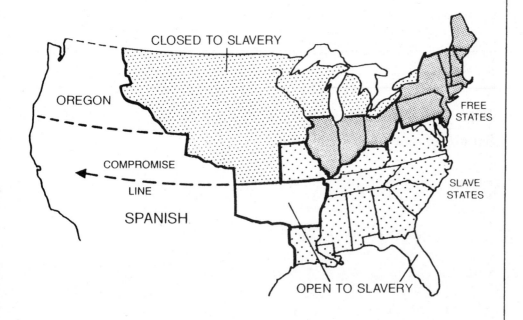

CLOSED TO SLAVERY

OREGON

COMPROMISE LINE

SPANISH

FREE STATES

SLAVE STATES

OPEN TO SLAVERY

Congress worked out the Missouri Compromise to make clear which states could have slavery and which could not.

Slaves were bought and sold at auctions, where people could bid for them. Families were often separated by a sale.

Getting Ready for Chapter Thirteen

13

Here are three vocabulary words that are used in the story about the quarrel between the North and South. Study these definitions so that you will know what each word means when you see it in your reading.

severely   (suh-VEER-lee) In a very harsh and stern way; strictly, painfully.

debate   (duh-BAYT) An argument between two or more speakers which follows special rules and is held in front of an audience.

oppose   (uh-POWZ) To be against.

The North and South Quarrel

Why weren't slaves allowed to go to school?
Who was Stephen A. Douglas?
What famous man was president at the time of the war between the North and the South?
What happened to John Brown?

When family members quarrel, their battling can sometimes do a lot of *damage*. In the 1800s, the North and the South, members of the American family, couldn't agree on anything important. These two parts of the United States finally had a fight that is one of the most important things that ever happened in this country. •

DAM-ij

Many Southern whites felt that slavery was *necessary* to a strong economy. Slaves worked hard on Southern farms. Many Southerners owned slaves. Some slaves were treated well by their masters, but many others were not. If the owners thought they were working too slowly, they whipped them. Some slaves were punished even more **severely**.

NEH-seh-sair-ee

Slaves were also kept from learning to read and write. They could not go to school. Their owners were afraid that education might make them fight for a better life. Many times slave families were broken up. Mothers or fathers were taken away from their children and sold to other owners. Slaves were thought of as property rather than as human beings.

There weren't many slaves in the North. More and more people there were beginning to feel that slavery was wrong. The Northern states passed laws against it. Instead, they paid white workers low *wages* to work in factories.

WAY-jez

When Southern slaves rose up against their masters, Northerners cheered. Slave owners told the North to mind its own business. •

Meanwhile, the United States was growing fast. New states west of the Mississippi River were being added to the Union. The South wanted to spread slavery into the new states. The North said the states should be free. Each side tried to get more states than the other. They were both afraid that the side with the most states would gain control of Congress and the government.

To settle the argument, Congress drew a line across a map of the Western states. All new states north of the southern border of *Missouri* would be free. All new states south of the line could have slavery. This agreement was called the Missouri Compromise. It kept the North and South from fighting from 1820 until 1854.

miz-UR-ee

In 1854, Kansas and Nebraska asked to become states. Both were north of the Missouri Compromise line. The North expected them to come in as free states. But Senator Douglas of *Illinois* had other ideas.

il-ih-NOY

Stephen A. Douglas was a Northerner. He hoped to become president of the United States some day. So he decided to make some friends in the South.

Douglas said it was not fair for Congress to decide whether states could have slaves or not. He thought it was up to the people in the states themselves to decide. For a while everyone thought this was a good idea. The people in Kansas and Nebraska were told to vote on the slavery problem.

Immediately, people from both the North and the South rushed to Kansas. Each side set up its own government. Fighting broke out, and five Northerners were killed. In revenge, Northerners murdered five Southerners. They were led by a man named John Brown. Brown hated slavery and spent his life fighting against it. •

ih-MEE-dee-ut-lee

The problem of slavery came to the Supreme Court in 1857. Dred Scott was a slave who had been taken to a free state by his master. Scott claimed that this made him free. But the United States Supreme Court decided against him. It said that slaves were not citizens; they were property. So Scott had no rights. Slaves could now be taken anywhere, even into free states.

The North was furious at the Court decision in the Dred Scott case. Angry citizens joined the *Republican* party. The Republicans said the spread of slavery must stop. Their leader was Abraham Lincoln, of Illinois.

ree-PUB-lih-kun

In 1858, Lincoln and Stephen A. Douglas, also of Illinois, held some **debates** on slavery. Lincoln disliked slavery much more than Douglas. He won many followers.

In 1859, John Brown led a surprise raid on Harper's Ferry, Virginia. Brown expected Southern slaves to join him in a *bloody* revolt against their masters. Instead, the United States Marines captured Brown, and he was put to death.

BLUD-ee

Northerners called John Brown a great hero. He had fought bravely to free the slaves. Southerners said Brown was a crazy trouble-maker. •

In 1860, Abraham Lincoln ran against Stephen Douglas for president of the United States. Southerners hated Lincoln because he **opposed** slavery. They warned that if Lincoln were elected, they would leave the Union. They would no longer be part of the United States.

Lincoln won the election and became president. Then the Southern states left the Union, just as they said they would. They formed a new government called the Confederate States of America. Jefferson Davis of Mississippi was elected president. North and South prepared for war.

Answer these to review the main ideas.

1. How were slaves treated in the South? _____
_____

   Why weren't slaves permitted to learn how to read and write? _____
_____

2. Why were the North and South fighting over slavery in the new western states? _____
_____

3. What was the Missouri Compromise? _____
_____

4. How did Stephen A. Douglas try to solve the problem of which states should be free and which slave? _____
_____

5. What did the Supreme Court say about the Dred Scott case? _____
_____
_____

6. Who was John Brown? _____
   What did he do? _____
_____

7. Why did the South hate Abraham Lincoln? _____
_____

   What did the South threaten to do if Lincoln was elected? _____
_____

Tell what happened on each of these dates. You may look back at the chapter if you need to.

1854 _____

1857 _____

1858 _____

1859 _____

1860 _____

Choose one of these words to fit each sentence below.

oppose   debate   severely

1. If two students are running against each other for president of the class, there may be a _____ before the election to give them a chance to say what they think.

2. Someone who commits a serious crime is often punished

   _____.

3. If we disagree strongly with someone's views, we _____ them.

Circle True or False.

T F 1. Southerners wanted their slaves to learn how to read and write.

T F 2. There were more slaves living in the North than in the South.

T F 3. Each side was afraid that the other would get more states and gain control of the federal government.

T F 4. The Republican party said that slavery must not be allowed to spread.

T F 5. Abraham Lincoln won the election of 1860 and became president of the United States.

Think about and discuss in class.

The Southern states called their new government the Confederate States of America. It was a *confederation* of states. What is a confederation? Check back in Chapters 1 and 2. How well did the United

States do under the Articles of Confederation? _____

_____

Does an educated person get along better in life than someone who is not educated? Who is likely to make more money — an educated person, or an uneducated one? Why? Would it be possible for you to be a slave

and to be happy at the same time? _____

_____

_____

If someone does you harm, is it right to get revenge? Was it right for

John Brown to murder five Southerners? _____

_____

_____

Americans have compromised on many problems, such as the kind of
government they would have. Why couldn't the North and South

compromise on slavery? _____

_____

_____

_____

_____

Northern and Southern armies fought for four years. The North was much larger than the South, but the South was fighting on its own land. Almost 200,000 Black soldiers fought for the North.

Getting Ready for Chapter Fourteen

14

Here are five vocabulary words that are used in the story about the Civil War. Study these definitions so that you will know what each word means when you see it in your reading.

civil war   (SIV-il)   A war between citizens of the same country.

creek   (KREEK)   A small stream. A brook.

spectator   (SPEK-tay-tur)   Someone who watches an event or a show without taking part.

discouraged   (dis-KUR-ijd)   To feel beaten and without hope.

encourage   (en-KUR-ij)   To give someone hope and confidence.

The four men at the left were
important leaders during the Civil
War. Top left: Abraham Lincoln
was the sixteenth president of the
United States. Bottom left: The
president of the Confederacy was
Jefferson Davis. Top right:
General Ulysses Grant led the
Northern armies to victory.
Bottom right: Robert E. Lee was
a Southern general and a great
leader.

THE CIVIL WAR — NORTH AGAINST SOUTH

Because of the Civil War the
eleven Southern states stayed in
the Union and slavery was ended.

The Civil War

Why didn't the South trust President Lincoln?
What happened at the Battle of Bull Run?
Who won the Civil War?

President Lincoln was sorry to see the South leave the Union and form its own government. He made a last try for peace. He would let the South keep its slaves if it would remain part of the United States. "We are not enemies, but friends," Lincoln told the South. "We must not be enemies."

But the South did not trust Lincoln. He had said many times that he thought slavery was wrong. He had said that slavery must not be allowed to grow. ●

The **Civil War** began in the harbor of Charleston, South Carolina, in 1861. Federal (Northern) troops held Fort Sumter, which was on a small *island* there. The Confederates (Southerners) blasted the fort with big cannons. As crowds on the shore watched and cheered, the North surrendered. That was the beginning of four terrible years of war.

EYE-lund

The capital of the new Southern government was Richmond, Virginia. A Northern army marched toward Richmond, expecting to beat the Southerners easily. Government officials and their wives brought along picnic lunches. They wanted to watch the fun when the Yankees chased the Southern *rebels* away.

REH-bulz

The two armies met at a **creek** called Bull Run. But it was the Rebels who did the chasing. They broke through the lines of the Northern soldiers and sent the Yankees running. They fled back to Washington, a distance of thirty miles. The **spectators** ran too, leaving their picnic lunches behind them. ●

The North was much larger than the South. It had more states and more people. It had more factories to make guns and supplies. But the South was fighting on its own land. Southern soldiers were protecting their own homes and families. This made them fight like tigers. And the South had good generals, especially Robert E. Lee. Time after time, Lee defeated the Northern armies.

The people in the North became **discouraged**. "What's the use of fighting?" they asked. "Let the South go. Let them have their slaves."

England and France were friendly to the South. It looked as if England might enter the war. In that case, the North would *surely* be beaten. President Lincoln decided that something had to be done to **encourage** the North. Millions of Northerners hated slavery. Lincoln sent them a message.

SHOOR-lee

Starting in 1863, Lincoln said, the North would be fighting for more than just keeping the South in the Union. It would also fight to free the slaves in the South. He invited Blacks everywhere to join the great *crusade* for freedom. ●

kroo-SAYD

Lincoln's words worked like magic. They did more good than winning a battle. Northerners got new hope and courage. Slaves escaped from the South and joined the *Union*, or Northern, armies and all-Black regiments were formed. Free Blacks in the North also joined up. The Confederates were hurt by Lincoln's message.

YOON-yun

England changed its mind about helping the South. English workers praised Lincoln for trying to free the slaves. The South's hope of getting help from England was gone.

Years of hard and bloody fighting remained, though. In July 1863, General Lee invaded Pennsylvania. He hoped to capture Philadelphia and Washington. The North would then surrender, he thought.

The Union Army met Lee at the town of *Gettysburg* in Pennsylvania. For three days the North and South fought there. Finally, Lee had to retreat. The South never threatened the North again.

GET-eez-burg

President Lincoln had a good general named *Ulysses* S. Grant. Grant had captured several Southern cities and forts out West along the Mississippi River. Now he was brought east to fight Lee.

yoo-LISS-eez

Grant had many more men than Lee, and he moved toward Richmond. The North lost thousands of soldiers, but Grant kept fighting. Finally Lee had almost no army left. He surrendered at *Appomattox*, Virginia, in 1865.

a-puh-MAT-iks

The Civil War was over. After four years the North had kept the eleven Southern states from leaving the Union. The slaves had been freed. Many problems remained to be solved. But at last, peace had returned to the country, and it became again the United States of America.

Answer these to review the main ideas.

A.

1. How did President Lincoln try to avoid a war with the South? ＿＿＿＿

＿＿＿＿＿＿＿＿＿＿＿＿＿＿＿＿＿＿＿＿＿＿＿＿＿＿＿＿＿＿＿

2. Why didn't the South accept Lincoln's offer of peace? ＿＿＿＿＿＿＿

＿＿＿＿＿＿＿＿＿＿＿＿＿＿＿＿＿＿＿＿＿＿＿＿＿＿＿＿＿＿＿

3. How did President Lincoln encourage the North to keep fighting?

＿＿＿＿＿＿＿＿＿＿＿＿＿＿＿＿＿＿＿＿＿＿＿＿＿＿＿＿＿＿＿

4. What part did England take in the Civil War? _____

_____

5. What did General Grant do to end the war?_____

_____

6. What two goals did the North win in the Civil War?_____

_____

B.

Circle the right answer to finish each sentence.

1. The Civil War began in the harbor of

   a. Boston   b. New York   c. Charleston

2. The Southern capital was

   a. Richmond,   b. Mobile,   c. Baltimore,
       Virginia   Alabama   Maryland

3. The North expected to win an easy victory at the Battle of

   a. Charleston   b. Bull Run   c. Fort Sumter

4. For a while it looked as if the South would get help from

   a. Spain   b. Mexico   c. England

5. Northern soldiers were sometimes called

   a. Rebels   b. Federals   c. Confederates

6. The Confederates were

   a. Southerners   b. Northerners   c. Yankees

C.

Circle True or False.

T   F   1. President Lincoln told the South that the North and South should be friends.

T   F   2. The South liked Lincoln because he said that slavery should be allowed to grow.

T   F   3. President Lincoln said that beginning in 1863, the North would fight to free the slaves in the South.

T   F   4. General Lee had more soldiers than General Grant.

T   F   5. The North's two goals were to keep the South in the Union and to free the Southern slaves.

Choose one of these words to fit each sentence below.

creek   encourage   discouraged   spectator   civil war

1. A small stream or body of running water is a _____ .

2. When fighting between two groups of citizens breaks out in a country, it is called a _____ .

3. If a baseball team loses one game after another, it easily becomes

   _____ .

4. It is fun to go to the ball park and be a _____ at an exciting game.

5. If we feel sad or hopeless, we sometimes can use someone to

   _____ us.

Think about and discuss in class.

There were several all-Black regiments in the Civil War, the most famous of which was the Massachusetts 54th Regiment. These regiments were made up of escaped slaves and free Blacks who volunteered to serve in the Union army. If you were a Black during the Civil War would you have volunteered? Why or why not? _____

_____

_____

Who do you think was the better general, General Lee or General Grant? Why? _____

_____

_____

Abraham Lincoln fought the war with words as well as with soldiers and guns. Can you explain what this means? _____

_____

Suppose Presidents Lincoln and Davis, and Generals Grant and Lee, could come back to visit the United States today. What would they think about the condition of Blacks in the United States? _____

_____

_____

Final Review Test

Here are fifteen vocabulary words you have learned while reading this book. Choose one word to fit each sentence below.

neutral	patriot	encourage
republic	compromise	debate
frontier	confederation	reform
spectator	territory	pioneer
immigrant	inaugurate	federation

1. A person who loves his or her country very much is a

   _____.

2. A country that has a president is a _____.

3. A person who watches a game or a show without taking part is a

   _____.

4. Countries or states working together but keeping their own inde-

   pendence are called a _____.

5. To get rid of faults and make improvements is called

   _____.

6. A partly settled area of land belonging to a government is a

   _____.

7. To give people hope and confidence when they need it is to

   _____ them.

8. Not taking either side in a fight or war is being _____.

9. States that work together under a strong central government are

   called a _____.

10. A person from another country who comes to America to live is

    an _____.

11. When two sides settle an argument by each giving in a little, they

    make a _____.

12. A person who moves into new or unsettled lands is a
_____.

13. Every four years, when the United States swears in a president, it
_____s him.

14. A formal argument between two speakers in front of an audience
is a _____.

15. The border between a developed area and the wilderness beyond
it is called the _____.

II. **Circle the right answer to finish each sentence.**

1. The American colonies fought for independence from

   a. France   b. Spain   c. England

2. George Washington became our first president in

   a. 1776   b. 1789   c. 1800

3. The United States bought the Louisiana Territory from

   a. Spain   b. England   c. France

4. "The Star-Spangled Banner" was written during the

   a. American   b. War of 1812   c. Mexican War
   Revolution

5. A dictator is

   a. someone who   b. the ruler of a   c. the head of a
   dictates into a   government in   democracy
   machine   which the people
                              have no say

6. Federal laws are made by

   a. the president   b. Congress   c. the states

7. "Old Hickory" was a nickname for

   a. James Madison   b. Andrew Jackson   c. Davy Crockett

8. The first telegraph was built by

   a. Samuel F. B. Morse b. Robert Fulton   c. Eli Whitney

9. The fort at San Antonio where Texans fought to the last man was called

   a. Goliad   b. the Alamo   c. San Jacinto

10. The president of the United States during the Mexican War was

    a. James K. Polk   b. Santa Anna   c. Andrew Jackson

11. The Oregon country stretched all the way from Alaska south to

    a. Canada   b. California   c. New Mexico

12. Gold was discovered in 1848 on the property of

    a. Sam Houston   b. Stephen Austin   c. John Sutter

13. Abraham Lincoln ran against Stephen Douglas for president in

    a. 1860   b. 1840   c. 1820

14. The Southern capital in the Civil War was

    a. Charleston, South Carolina   b. New Orleans, Louisiana   c. Richmond, Virginia

III.

Circle True or False

T   F   1. George Washington was the first president of the United States.

T   F   2. Every state, large or small, has two senators in the United States Senate.

T   F   3. Our first six presidents all came from western states.

T   F   4. Southerners said that their slaves were better off than the women and children who worked in northern factories.

T   F   5. Americans everywhere were strongly in favor of war with Mexico.

T   F   6. California did not become a state until 1900.

T   F   7. There were more slaves living in the North than in the South.

IV.

T   F   8. In the Civil War the North wanted to keep the South in the Union and to free the Southern slaves.

Find the definition that matches each word and write the letter on the line.

_____ president of the United States   a. built missions in California

_____ Rio Grande   b. changes in the Constitution

_____ California   c. tried to help slaves

_____ amendments   d. invented cotton gin

_____ Santa Anna   e. "Bear Flag Republic"

_____ Father Junipero Serra   f. Mexican general and president

_____ John Brown   g. where Civil War started

_____ Eli Whitney   h. slave who claimed freedom

_____ Fort Sumter   i. commander-in-chief of armed forces

_____ Dred Scott   j. river on Mexican border

V.

In your own words, write about an American you read about in this book who helped his or her country. The person could be a president, a soldier, an explorer, or a leader. Use this book to help you.